STUDY GUIDE

ISRAEL

AND THE

CHURCH

AMIR
TSARFATI

HARVEST HOUSE PUBLISHERS
EUGENE, OREGON

Cover design by Kyler Dougherty

Cover photo (c) sommthink, revers, Rich Carey, alfocome, Didecs / Shutterstock; tzahiv / Gettyimage

Interior design by KUHN Design Group

For bulk, special sales, or ministry purchases, please call 1-800-547-8979.
Email: Customerservice@hhpbooks.com

M is a federally registered trademark of the Hawkins Children's LLC. Harvest House Publishers, Inc., is the exclusive licensee of the trademark.

Israel and the Church Study Guide
Copyright © 2021 by Amir Tsarfati
Published by Harvest House Publishers
Eugene, Oregon 97408
www.harvesthousepublishers.com

ISBN 978-0-7369-8272-6 (pbk.)
ISBN 978-0-7369-8273-3 (eBook)

Printed in the United States of America

21 22 23 24 25 26 27 28 29 / BP-SK / 10 9 8 7 6 5 4 3 2 1

CONTENTS

PART 1: TWO CHOSEN PEOPLES

PART 2: TWO DISTINCT PLANS

PART 3: TWO PATHS IN REVELATION

PART 4: TWO PEOPLES, ONE FAMILY

PART 1:

TWO
CHOSEN
PEOPLES

LESSON 1

FEAR NOT

"We must understand the truth of God's presence in the midst of the imperfect times. God didn't create the imperfect. God doesn't cause the imperfect. But God works through the imperfect. That's who He is. He is a perfect God who carries out His perfect will in imperfect people who live in an imperfect world. When God first created this universe, everything was perfect. The perfect God established His perfect creation by His perfect Word. Then humanity expressed the free will with which the Lord had gifted it, and everything blew apart. Sin entered the world, and with sin came death. Creation was separated from Creator."

Israel and the Church, pages 16-17

As the world all around us continues to decline morally and spiritually, it's easy to become discouraged. With evil running rampant, we may feel as though there is no hope. All of this is a result of sin's entrance into the world. With sin comes separation from God, which, in turn, brings corruption, decay, wickedness, and ultimately, death.

As Scripture says, "The whole world lies under the sway of the wicked one" (1 John 5:19). Satan is "the prince of the power of the air, the spirit who works in the sons of disobedience" (Ephesians 2:2). This is why we are given the warning to "be sober, be vigilant; because your adversary the devil walks about like a roaring lion, seeking whom he may devour" (1 Peter 5:8).

Yet God does not want us to live in fear. All through Scripture, He has given us many reminders of the hope we have as believers. The more we read His Word, the more confidence we have that no matter how bad things get, God is still in control. And He has already secured the victory that assures us of a future totally free from sin, a future in which all will be perfect again.

A NEED FOR HOPE

First Peter 1:3 says, "Blessed be the God and Father of our Lord Jesus Christ, who according to His abundant mercy has begotten us again to a living hope through the resurrection of Jesus Christ from the dead."

What does the passage say God is abundant in?

What has God "begotten us again to"?

What do the words "living hope" tell us about the kind of hope we have?

What makes this hope possible?

Romans 15:4 tells us, "Whatever things were written before were written for our learning, that we through the patience and comfort of the Scriptures might have hope."

For what purposes did God give His Word to us?

In what ways have you received hope during your most recent readings of the Bible?

Why do you think it is so important for us to keep our eyes on the hope God has given us?

In 2 Corinthians 4:16-18, Paul wrote, "We do not lose heart.

Even though our outward man is perishing, yet the inward man is being renewed day by day. For our light affliction, which is but for a moment, is working for us a far more exceeding and eternal weight of glory, while we do not look at the things which are seen, but at the things which are not seen. For the things which are seen are temporary, but the things which are not seen are eternal."

For what reasons did Paul say "we do not lose heart"?

How does Paul describe our affliction, then our glory?

What are we called to look at?

In 2 Corinthians 4:16-18, Paul reveals to us the power of keeping our focus on that which is eternal. As believers, we are to look heavenward. That is why so much of the Bible is filled with prophecy. The more we read prophecy, the more our hope increases. In this way, we can replace our fears with hope.

GOD'S LONG-SUFFERING GRACE

Though sin separates us from God, He didn't give up on humanity. This is true for all people, including the Old Testament nation of Israel. Even though the people repeatedly rejected their Lord, He reached out to them, inviting them to return to Him. Even in their unfaithfulness, God pleaded,

> You have burdened Me with your sins,
> You have wearied Me with your iniquities.
> I, even I, am He who blots out your transgressions
>   for my own sake;
> And I will not remember your sins.
> Put Me in remembrance;
> Let us contend together;
> State your case that you may be acquitted
>   (Isaiah 43:24-26).

God did not abandon Israel. We can take great comfort in that, for if He has long-suffering patience for the Jewish people, then He will show that same patience to us today even when we fail Him.

Hosea 3:4-5 says, "The children of Israel shall abide many days without king or prince, without sacrifice or sacred pillar, without ephod or teraphim. Afterward the children of Israel shall return and seek the Lord their God and David their king. They shall fear the Lord and His goodness in the latter days."

After a time without king or prince, what will the people of Israel do?

What will Israel do "in the latter days"?

Do you see this prophecy as one that offers hope to Israel? Why?

About three decades after the church had been born, Paul wrote the book of Romans. What did he say about the Jewish people in Romans 11:1?

What did Paul later add in Romans 11:29? Will God ever go back on His promises?

How is God's love for Israel described in Jeremiah 31:3?

What do the above passages tell you about God's commitment to Israel?

THE POWERFUL PRESENCE OF GOD

One vitally important fact we must understand about God's love for His people is that just because He disciplines them doesn't mean He will abandon them. When God disciplined the nation of Israel, He did so out of love; His desire was to get the people's attention so they would return to Him. The hand that disciplines is the same hand that restores and protects. We see this clearly in Isaiah 43, where God warns Israel that punishment is about to come, yet that doesn't mean He will abandon His people.

Read Isaiah 43:2. What promise did God make to the people of Israel before they were attacked by the powerful Assyrians?

What assurance does God give in Isaiah 43:5?

When God disciplines, He does so out of love—in the same way a loving parent disciplines a wayward child. Hebrews

11:5-6 says, "Do not despise the chastening of the LORD, nor be discouraged when you are rebuked by Him; for whom the LORD loves He chastens."

In what way can we say that rebuke or chastening is evidence of love?

In what ways have you seen God's discipline in your own life be beneficial for you?

A PROVEN FAITHFULNESS

Read Nehemiah 9:5-15, and list all the ways you see God's faithfulness demonstrated to Israel from the time of Abraham to Nehemiah.

In Psalm 77, Asaph said, "In the day of my trouble I sought the Lord...I am so troubled that I cannot speak...Has His mercy ceased forever? Has His promise failed forevermore?" (verses 2,4,8). He thought God had abandoned him. Then we see a change of heart in verses 10-15. What happened, according to verses 11-12?

What does Asaph credit God with doing in verses 14-15?

THE DAY OF SALVATION

> "When you open your heart to the love and forgiveness of Jesus Christ, He will make you a new person. He will spark a light in you—a light of new life, a light of eternity. Then He will use that light in you to shine His truth to the world."
>
> *Israel and the Church*, page 24

Read Romans 1:16. What does Paul say the gospel has the power to do?

And who is the gospel available to?

The church had its beginning in Jerusalem in Acts 2, and many of the first believers were Jews. After Paul became a believer, he traveled far and wide to proclaim the gospel. According to Acts 17:1-2, what was Paul's custom each time he traveled to a new town?

What does this custom reveal about God's perspective regarding the Jewish people—a perspective that continues through today?

As Christians, we're called to share the gospel to all people, no matter what their background. How does God's faithfulness to Israel serve as an example to you with regard to your thoughts about and interactions with Jewish people?

Taking This Lesson to Heart

What truth or principle had the greatest impact on you in chapter 1 of *Israel and the Church*?

In this chapter, we learned a lot about God's faithfulness. What do you appreciate most about this characteristic of God?

Take a moment now to pray, both praising and thanking God for His love, patience, and mercy in your life.

LESSON 2

TWO TRUMPETS ARE BETTER THAN ONE

"Occasionally in the Bible, God will introduce a person or event or item that we will later discover has more significance than we originally anticipated. These are sometimes called types or representations or shadows. In my previous book, *The Day Approaching*, I presented the Old Testament feasts as shadow celebrations representing greater future events. For example, Passover found its fulfillment in the crucifixion of Christ. The Feast of Unleavened Bread was satisfied in the perfect, sinless life of the Bread of Life, Jesus Christ. The Feast of Firstfruits was a shadow of the resurrection of our Lord, whom Paul describes as "the firstfruits of those who have fallen asleep" (1 Corinthians 15:20), indicating that we, too, will one day rise up in like manner from the grave. The Feast of Weeks, remembered over Pentecost, was expressed when the Holy Spirit was poured out upon the church. The Feast of Trumpets is finding current fulfillment in the signs all around us announcing the soon coming of our Lord. The Day of Atonement and the Feast of Tabernacles or Booths are still awaiting their realities, when, respectively, all Israel comes to Christ and when the church and all who follow the Lord will dwell together with Him in the millennial kingdom. For each of these events, something lesser is established that will find its greater counterpart in the future."

Israel and the Church, page 31

In Scripture, a type or shadow is a representation of something to come. It's a picture that is meant to illustrate a future reality. To get a better idea of what this means, let's look at one of the most prominent examples in Scripture.

Read Genesis 22:7-8. What did Abraham tell Isaac that God would provide for the burnt offering?

According to Exodus 12:3-13, what were the Israelites to offer up as a sacrifice to protect their firstborn from death?

In the Old Testament prophetic passage Isaiah 53:7, what was Christ likened to with regard to His future crucifixion?

How did John the Baptist describe Jesus in John 1:29?

In multiple Old Testament passages, a sacrificial lamb points to the future Messiah who would be slaughtered for our transgressions so that we could receive God's forgiveness. This is just one example of the many types or representations we can find in Scripture.

In chapter 2 of *Israel and the Church*, we focus on how the two silver trumpets in Numbers 10:1-10 serve as a type.

A SHADOW OF SOMETHING GREATER

According to Numbers 10:2, what was the purpose of the two silver trumpets?

As stated on pages 32-33 of *Israel and the Church*, what were the four primary ways trumpets could be used to inform the Israelites of what to do?

For what event do we see a trumpet used in 1 Thessalonians 4:16-17?

And what event is a trumpet used for in Matthew 24:29-31?

A CALL TO ATTENTION

Distractions are one of Satan's great tools against us. What are some examples of distractions that have caused you to remove your eyes from God?

A key purpose of the trumpets in the Old Testament was to warn and alert people. To better understand what these trumpets look like to us today, what must we first recognize (see page 35 in *Israel and the Church*)?

God's First Trumpet: Israel

In Genesis 12:1-3, did Abraham choose God, or did God choose Abraham?

In this passage, do we see any indication at all that Abraham had done something worthy that would cause God to select him?

What was God's purpose for Israel, according to Isaiah 43:10?

Read Deuteronomy 7:6-7. What does God say about His reason for making Israel His chosen people?

How does God describe the Israelites in Deuteronomy 9:4-7? Had the people done anything that made them deserve the Promised Land?

God's Second Trumpet: The Church

What is the purpose of the church, according to Matthew 28:19-20 and Acts 1:8?

Read Ephesians 2:8-9 and Titus 3:5. Have we as Christians done anything to deserve the honor of pointing people to God and proclaiming the message of salvation in Christ?

God is sovereign and can choose whomever He wishes to serve as His witnesses. What does it say about the nature of God's love that He is so willing to work through imperfect vessels?

The primary messages of Israel and the church are different. What did God expect Israel to announce?

What primary message is the church to focus on?

A DEEPER LOOK

God commanded that only two silver trumpets be made. What does the number two represent?

In what do both Israel and the church find their origin?

When will the union of Israel and the church come?

What is significant about the fact the trumpets were made of silver rather than gold?

Ultimately, whose breath passes through the trumpets of Israel and the church?

Do you agree that "it is only when the breath of God passes through [Israel and the church] that they will play as He wants them to play"? Why?

What is the source of God's breath in our lives, according to 1 Corinthians 3:16?

What is our other source of life-supporting and witness-giving breath, according to 2 Timothy 3:16-17?

Why are so many churches sounding foul notes today?

WHAT SOUND ARE YOU MAKING?

"We are called to alert the lost about who God is and what is about to happen. The only way we can make sure that our sound is loud and our notes are true is to be daily in the Word of God and in prayer. This will allow the Spirit of God to fill our minds and His breath to fill our lungs. That is when all those around us will hear the trumpets of God in all we say and do."

Israel and the Church, page 42

In the Old Testament, God chose the nation of Israel to serve as witnesses, as messengers that would call people to attention and warn them of their need to seek God. Today, God speaks through the church. Christians are the trumpet God is using to make Himself known.

When it comes to the sound you're making, could you be doing better? What are some specific ways you can improve as a messenger?

Do you agree that spending time (1) in prayer and (2) in God's Word would make you a better trumpet? Why?

Taking This Lesson to Heart

What truth or principle had the greatest impact on you in chapter 2 of *Israel and the Church*?

God has chosen Christians to serve as His messengers to the world. What is the basic content of that message? What are some ways you can make sure you're a good messenger?

What weighs most heavily on your heart about your responsibility as a trumpet to the people around you? Take time to pray about this—ask God to help you fulfill this role in a way that people can hear His truth clearly through you.

LESSON 3

GETTING THE FULL PICTURE

"One of the great misunderstandings of the Jewish people and the church is that God chose Israel because of who Israel was. It's as if God looked ahead at the descendants of Abraham and was stunned and amazed. He decided that these future generations would be such wonderful examples of holiness and righteousness that they deserved His blessings to be poured out on them. However, as we saw earlier, the choosing of the Jewish people was less for that single nation than it was for the rest of the nations. God selected Israel with the intent that they would become His vessel for approaching the rest of the world with His truth and salvation.

"This same purpose also applies to the church. Being a Christian has less to do with our own eternity than it does the eternities of others. We are certainly blessed with the promise of heaven in our future and God's presence in the here and now. But if that's where our perspective of Christianity ends, then we are missing God's greater plan and His calling for us. We are saved for a purpose. We are saved for service. Israel was God's way to reflect Himself to the world. The church is His chosen vessel to tell the world the good news that Jesus Christ has paid the price for their sins."

Israel and the Church, pages 45-46

A GOD OF SECOND CHANCES

In Exodus 9:16, God tells Pharaoh, "For this purpose I have raised you up, that I may show My power in you, and that My name may be declared in all the earth."

Why did God raise up Pharaoh?

In Ezekiel 6, God tells the prophet Ezekiel that He will bring judgment upon Israel for her idolatry. Why did he do this, according to verse 7?

In 1 Kings 8, when King Solomon dedicated the Temple in Jerusalem, he spoke to the nation of Israel. What did he say about God in verses 56-57?

What is the main purpose of God's promises to Israel, according to verse 60?

Isn't it interesting to note that all people would know "that the Lord is God" in times of Israel's obedience *as well as* disobedience? Either way, God's character is visibly on display to everyone. What attributes of God does the world see manifest in the times that Israel—and the church—are *obedient*?

What attributes does the world see on display in the times when Israel—as well as the church—are *disobedient*?

In Isaiah 46:9-10, we read, "I am God, and there is none like Me...saying, 'My counsel shall stand, and I will do all My pleasure.'" Nothing can stand in God's way—He will do what He determines to do. And yet even when His people rebel, God does not abandon His children.

What do we learn about God in Exodus 34:6?

In Micah 7:18?

What future promise did God give to Israel in Ezekiel 36:24-28?

What did the apostle Peter do in John 18:15-17,25-27?

How do we see Jesus respond to Peter's betrayal (see John 21:15-19)?

What promise does God give to all believers in 1 John 1:9?

For both Israel and the church, God is indeed a God of second chances! Give an example of how you have experienced this in your own life:

THE STEADFAST
LOVE OF THE FATHER

Some people say that because Israel failed in its role as messenger for God, He is finished with them. But that is contrary to what we see in Scripture.

According to Romans 3:28-30, who is God "the God of"? What two groups of people is God willing to justify?

What does Paul tell us in Romans 11:1-2?

Read Romans 11:11-12. Why should Gentile Christians be thanking the Jews? And what are the Jews to be provoked to as a result?

How do we see God's purposes at work in both Israel and the Gentiles in Romans 11:25-26?

GOD HAS APPOINTED THE TIMES

What does Ecclesiastes 3:1 tell us God has done?

What does the fact God has planned "every purpose under heaven" tell you about Him?

What does Galatians 4:4-5 reveal to us about Christ's birth?

Why should we be encouraged by the fact God is so precise about how His plans unfold?

In light of what you have learned so far about God's love and His plans, do you think God wasted His time when He chose the Old Testament nation of Israel to be His messenger? Why?

As we read Scripture, anytime we see the words "so that," what should we remember?

As an example, what three "that" clauses do we see in John 3:16-17?

In all this, we see that God is very intentional—He knows exactly what He is doing. We might not understand His plan or purposes, but we can trust Him. In what ways do you find this assurance helpful for you personally?

SATAN'S LOSING STRATEGY

Satan knows he is a defeated foe. However, he is still determined to do all he can to disrupt God's plan for the salvation of Israel. What is Satan's end goal, according to Psalm 83:4?

Read Zechariah 2:8. When someone chooses to fight against Israel, who else are they fighting against?

What does the fact God has preserved the people of Israel all through the ages—even in times of severe persecution—tell us about Him?

Read John 10:28-29 and Romans 8:35-39. What specifically do these passages tell us about the security of the believer?

GOD IS FAITHFUL
EVEN WHEN WE AREN'T

"The fact that God is still faithful to Israel despite the people's unbelieving state demonstrates the marvelous character of our Lord. Too many people focus on the unfaithfulness of Israel instead of on the faithfulness of God. In fact, it just might be that Israel is more effective at showing the glory of who our God is in their rebellion than they ever were when they were faithful."

Israel and the Church, page 58

Read Romans 3:3-4. Does the fact the Jewish people chose to reject Christ cancel the faithfulness of God (see pages 57-58 in *Israel and the Church*)?

In Genesis 17:7-8, what key word describes the nature of God's covenant to Israel?

Consider the statement, "God is faithful—He cannot deny Himself. His love for His children is based solely on His character, not on our actions." What is your response to this truth, and why?

Taking This Lesson to Heart

What truth or principle had the greatest impact on you in chapter 3 of *Israel and the Church*?

The fact God is faithful to His own should inspire us, out of love, to be faithful in response. How can we demonstrate our faithfulness to Him?

How has this lesson deepened your appreciation for God? As you consider the answer, give prayerful thanks to the Lord for the ways He cares for Israel, the church, and you.

PART 2:

TWO DISTINCT PLANS

LESSON 4

A WIFE AND A BRIDE

"Divorce is a serious undertaking and its ramifications can be widespread and devastating. This is why it is so jarring to read God say, 'Then I saw that for all the causes for which backsliding Israel had committed adultery, I had put her away and given her a certificate of divorce' (Jeremiah 3:8). God divorced His chosen people. No matter how bad they were, was there anything that they could have done that would demand that severe of a response? In a word, yes. Big time. In fact, the long-suffering patience of the Lord is the only reason it hadn't happened much sooner. Israel was unfaithful to her Husband in innumerable and extreme ways. So God said, 'Because of your unfaithfulness, our marriage is at an end.'

"Sadly, there are many people who say that's when Israel's story finished. 'See,' they say, 'God put aside Israel for good. In their place, He found a more faithful bride—the church.' But they say this because either they have never read their whole Bible, or they don't understand the true character of God—or both. The Father sent Israel away, but for a reason and only for a season. And in His time, He will once again be united to His wife in a union that will last for eternity."

Israel and the Church, pages 63-64

SET APART FOR GOD

In what way did God call His people to be set apart in Leviticus 20:26?

List three or four additional ways God called His people to distinguish themselves, according to Leviticus chapter 19. Note especially verses 3-4 and 37. Why would God want the Israelites to stand out from the nations that surrounded them?

What exhortation is given to Christians in Romans 12:2?

For what purpose are we set aside, according to 1 Peter 2:9?

According to Galatians 5:16, what additional reason do we have to be set apart?

What clear command does Jesus give us in Matthew 5:13-14?

In what ways can we ensure we are useful as salt and light?

The more we make sure God is visible in our lives, the more people will have opportunity to be drawn toward Him and discover Him.

THE GOD WHO KEEPS ISRAEL

What proclamation do we find in Psalm 121:4?

For greater context, read all of Psalm 121. What other assurances does God give?

How long will God preserve His own, according to the end of verse 8?

"God's plan has always been to let the nations see who He is through how He handles Israel" (*Israel and the Church*, page 67). What conclusion can we come to when we consider that, after 2,000 years of being spread through all the

nations, the Jewish people are back in their own land again—
and their culture and language have returned as well?

According to Romans 9:4-5, what are some of the gifts that
God gave to the Jews, and, in turn, gave to the rest of the
world?

Romans 9:5 tells us that it was through the Jews that "Christ
came." Now read Genesis 12:1-3, especially verse 3. What
was God's ultimate purpose for making the Israelites His
chosen people?

Nearly 2,000 years went by from the time God spoke Genesis 12:1-3 to the time when Christ died on the cross and rose
again to accomplish God's plan to make salvation possible.
Considering all the twists and turns that happened along
the way, what does this tell you about God's sovereignty?

What confidence does this give you regarding God's sovereignty over the future?

ADDING TO, NOT REPLACING

Romans 11:16-18 says,

> If the firstfruit is holy, the lump is also holy; and if the root is holy, so are the branches. And if some of the branches were broken off, and you, being a wild olive tree, were grafted in among them, and with them became a partaker of the root and fatness of the olive tree, do not boast against the branches. But if you do boast, remember that you do not support the root, but the root supports you.

In this passage, note that the "wild olive tree"—that is, the church—is "grafted in" to the original olive tree, or Israel. Does that imagery tell us that the church has *replaced* Israel, or that it has been *added* to Israel?

According to the final words in the passage, what is the church's relationship to the root (that is, Israel)?

WHEN ALL ARE ONE IN CHRIST

Some people point to Galatians 3:28 and Ephesians 2:15 as evidence that the Jews are no longer distinctly God's chosen people and have been replaced by the church. Let's look at each passage carefully:

Galatians 3:28—"There is neither Jew nor Greek, there is neither slave nor free, there is neither male nor female; for you are all one in Christ Jesus."

Is there anything in the verse that actually states the Jews have been *replaced* by the church?

The actual point of the verse is this: No matter what our background, we are all _____ in Christ.

Ephesians 2:14-15—"He Himself is our peace, who has made both one, and has broken down the middle wall of separation, having abolished in His flesh the enmity, that is, the law of commandments contained in ordinances, so as to create in Himself one new man from the two, thus making peace."

Up until Christ's death on the cross, Jews and Gentiles remained separated. But at the cross, Jesus disposed of the need to fulfill "the law of commandments," making access to God possible through His sacrifice—access that God made available to *both* Jews and the church. According to the final words of verse 15, what was the result of Christ's action on the cross?

Does this passage say, in any way, that the church has *replaced* Israel? What does it actually say has happened?

THE STREET GOES ONLY ONE WAY

When God makes the new heavens and new earth, why will there no longer be a need for either Israel or the church?

When a Jewish person receives Christ, he or she becomes a part of the church. But why should there be no reciprocal movement from the church to Judaism?

TWO KEY ILLUSTRATIONS

The Relationship Between God and Israel

What intimate relationship does Scripture use to portray God's relationship with Israel?

What warning did God give to Israel in Deuteronomy 6:14-15?

How did Israel (the wife) deal with God (her husband), according to Jeremiah 3:20?

Read Jeremiah 3:6-8. What did God do to Israel as a result of her backsliding?

Thankfully, that's not where the story ends. In summary, what did God say to Israel in Isaiah 62:1-5?

Note especially the ends of verses 4 and 5. What attitude will God show to Israel?

Read Jeremiah 31:31-33. Who will make the new covenant that is to come with "the house of Israel and with the house of Judah"?

Who broke the former covenant?

In verse 33, what promises does God give to "the house of Israel"?

The language in Jeremiah 31:31-33 clearly speaks of *restoration*, and not replacement. Those who broke the former covenant—that is, Israel—will be offered a new covenant.

The Relationship Between the Son and the Church

In Ephesians 5:25-27, what is Christ's relationship to the church likened to?

Why does Christ "sanctify and cleanse" the church?

Are we worthy of Christ's love? Explain.

In the same way that God chose to love undeserving Israel, God chooses to love us today. What response should we have to this extraordinary love?

A GOD OF RESTORATION

> "Through Israel and the church, we learn about God. We learn that He is jealous. But He is also loving and forgiving. He is the God of restoration and of reconciliation."
>
> *Israel and the Church*, page 79

What assurance does Hosea 6:1 offer to a broken and injured Israel?

A key part of God's future restoration promises is that the Jewish people would return to their homeland. Read Jeremiah 32:37-40. Because of His anger and wrath, God drove the Israelites into other countries. Then He clearly says, "I will bring them back to this place." This promise is made to the ones who were scattered—not to anyone else.

What does God then promise in verse 40?

How long will this covenant last?

In light of what you have learned, what words would you use to describe the love God shows to His chosen peoples— Israel and the church?

Taking This Lesson to Heart

What truth or principle had the greatest impact on you in chapter 4 of *Israel and the Church*?

Share about two or three ways you've experienced God's restoring love in your own life.

Take some time to pray and thank God for His everlasting and irrevocable love for you.

GOD'S TOUGH LOVE

"Israel was sin-addicted. What made it worse was that not only could the people not stop sinning, they had no desire to. They loved their sin. They relished it. They took sin to the next level, even outdoing the sins of all the nations around them…

"The Lord had had enough. The chances were now over. It was time for some tough love. He told the Israelites, 'I am going to bring some very difficult times your way. And then I am going to cut you off.' Just like a parent sometimes has to cut a child off to force them to change, God removed His hand from His children. No more blessings, no more protection, no more listening to their prayers, no more accepting of their halfhearted worship, and no more land. He was done with them, and they would now be on their own—broken, defeated, and homeless. But there was one hope they still had: God's beloved children will never cease to be God's beloved children."

Israel and the Church, pages 82-83

God sent numerous warnings to the nation of Israel. He sent multiple prophets over several centuries. If we start counting from the exodus (during which Israel wandered for 40 years in the wilderness) to the time the northern kingdom was taken captive by the Assyrians, that's approximately 700 years. Sometimes the people would return to Him for a while, but then they would backslide again. No one can accuse the Lord of lacking patience.

As Nehemiah said:

> Yet for many years You had patience with them, and testified against them by Your Spirit in Your prophets. Yet they would not listen; therefore You gave them into the hand of the peoples of the lands. Nevertheless in Your great mercy You did not utterly consume them nor forsake them; for You are God, gracious and merciful (9:30-31).

Even today, God continues to show patience.

A TIME OF DISCIPLINE

According to Ezekiel 5:6-8, what were the Israelites guilty of?

Read Ezekiel 5:15. For what key purpose did the Lord bring this punishment?

In the midst of all the judgment, what promise did God make in Ezekiel 6:8?

What will this remnant remember, according to verse 9?

The fact God would permit a remnant tells us that ultimately, God's beloved children will never cease to be His beloved children. That has been the story of Israel—there has always been a remnant. Even after the horrific judgment by Rome in AD 70, when Jerusalem and the Temple were destroyed and burned, there was a remnant.

When God's people fail Him, His work continues to move forward. As stated on page 84 of *Israel and the Church*, "What is a crisis of relationship to the _____ is an opportunity for growth in the _____."

To whom was the gospel message proclaimed, according to the following verses?

Matthew 10:5-6—

Matthew 15:24—

Luke 24:47—

Romans 1:16—

What was Paul's desire in Romans 10:1?

Though most of the Jews rejected the message of salvation from Jesus and the apostles, still, when the church was born, it was made up primarily of Jewish people who received Christ as Savior. Also, Paul's habit as a missionary was to preach in the synagogue in every town he visited during his travels, and some Jews did come to Christ. Though we are still seeing God's tough love in action today, He is still at work among the Jews, and there are many Jews today who have become believers. God's work has not stopped among the people of Israel.

What word of hope do we see for the Jewish people in Romans 2:10?

With regard to Jews and Gentiles, what truth is clearly stated in the very next verse?

Read Romans 11:4-5. According to verse 4, how many Old Testament Israelites did God say had *not* "bowed the knee to Baal" in the time of Elijah? In other words, how many had not fallen into idolatry?

In verse 5, what did God confirm to be true about the Jewish people at the time Paul wrote Romans?

This passage is yet another confirmation that all through the ages, God has had a remnant of the Jewish people who have stayed faithful to Him.

AN IRREVOCABLE CALLING

Read Romans 11:11. How is it that the gospel came to the Gentiles?

As the Jews see Gentiles coming to salvation, what will they be provoked to?

Read Romans 11:28-29. Note the words "concerning the election" in verse 28. What does verse 29 say about "the gifts and calling of God"?

What do the following passages say about God and His chosen people Israel?

1 Samuel 12:22—

1 Kings 6:13—

Psalm 89:31-37—

Psalm 94:14—

Isaiah 49:15—

Isaiah 54:10—

Once called by God, always called by God. That is true for both Israel and the church.

FIRST STEPS TO NATIONHOOD AGAIN

What did the Balfour Declaration do?

While the Balfour Declaration was a great first step, what did it lack?

What did the San Remo conference accomplish for Israel?

THE TIME IS COMING SOON

In the Old Testament era, at a certain corner of the Temple wall, a trumpet would be sounded at appointed times. Ultimately, what was the purpose of the trumpet soundings?

What, in essence, was the trumpet "sounded" at the Balfour Declaration saying?

What was the trumpet "sounded" at the San Remo convention saying?

What did the trumpet of the Holocaust proclaim?

What other historical events have, in effect, served as trumpets, as stated on page 91 of *Israel and the Church*?

Ezekiel 36:8-11 says,

> You, O mountains of Israel, you shall shoot forth your branches and yield your fruit to My people Israel, for they are about to come. For indeed I am for you, and I will turn to you, and you shall be tilled and sown. I will multiply men upon you, all the house of Israel, all of it; and the cities shall be inhabited and the ruins rebuilt. I will multiply upon you man and beast; and they shall increase and bear young; I will make you inhabited as in former times, and do better for you than at your beginnings. Then you shall know that I am the LORD.

In those verses, what specific promises did God give about Israel's future?

What do you see happening in Israel today that serves as confirmation that Ezekiel 36:8-11 is being fulfilled before our very eyes?

ARE YOU LISTENING?

"Every sound of the trumpet brings the world one step closer to the great tribulation. But it also brings every Christian one step closer to seeing Jesus' face."

Israel and the Church, page 93

The trumpets are sounding. The time is coming. How does that make you feel, and why?

Why can we as Christians legitimately say that even as the world is collapsing all around us, we are filled with hope and looking forward to the future?

In 1 Thessalonians 4:16-18, what did Paul say believers are to do to comfort one another?

In light of what you have learned in this chapter, why is it so important for the church to keep its eyes on what is happening in Israel today?

Taking This Lesson to Heart

What truth or principle had the greatest impact on you in chapter 5 of *Israel and the Church*?

In what ways have you gained a greater appreciation of God in this chapter?

A greater appreciation for Israel?

A greater appreciation for Bible prophecy?

Take time to pray now and express your newfound or deepened appreciations to the Lord.

GOD'S APPOINTED TIMES

"It often feels like time runs our lives. We have our appointments and our schedules. We know where we need to be and when we need to be there. If someone is punctual about showing up for meetings, we see that as a sign of good character. If someone is late, we feel disrespected and wonder if that person can be depended on in other areas of life. Time tells us when to go to bed and when to wake up. It sets the moment we need to be at work or when we have to drive the kids to soccer practice or when we must arrive at church so that we can be sure to get our usual seats.

"It is this dependence on time that has so many believers sitting at home with a stopwatch, thinking, *Okay, God, when is the rapture going to happen? You said soon, and by this point You're probably stretching the outer limits of even the most liberal definitions of that word. A day or even a week, that can still fit the 'soon' definition. But two thousand years feels a little excessive.* So Christians make predictions and set dates. But, as tough as it is for us to accept, when we ask God, 'When?,' His answer is typically, 'None of your business.'"

Israel and the Church, page 98

We *should* be eager for the Lord's return. And yet we must wait on God's perfect timing. What do we learn about God's timing in Romans 11:25?

What else do we learn about God's timing from 2 Peter 3:9?

In what other ways do we see confirmation of God's perfect timing with regard to His work over the course of time?

Genesis 18:14—

Ecclesiastes 3:1—

Ecclesiastes 3:17—

Habakkuk 2:3—

Mark 1:15—

Galatians 4:4-5—

1 Timothy 6:14-15—

THE ETERNAL GOD CREATED TIME
WHEN HE CREATED THE WORLD

According to Genesis 3:1-5, how did God begin defining time?

With regard to time, what did God establish in Exodus 12:2?

What measures of time do we see described in Genesis 8:22?

> "When God created, time began. He then took time and arranged it in an orderly fashion so that we could mark its passing. This is the system that now directs our days."
>
> *Israel and the Church*, page 100

GOD CREATED US WITHIN TIME

When did God insert part of Himself into His creation?

What did Jesus say about time in John 7:6 and 2:4?

What does this tell us about the Son's relationship to time?

What did King David say about time in Psalm 31:15?

According to the following passages, how much control do we have over our time?

Psalm 90:10—

Proverbs 27:1—

James 4:14—

What do these passages say about our lives in relation to time?

Job 14:5—

Psalm 31:15—

Psalm 139:16—

As a result, what attitude should we have?

Ephesians 5:15-16—

Colossians 4:5—

1 Peter 1:17—

OUR SOVEREIGN GOD HAS DETERMINED THE WHAT, WHEN, AND WHERE OF ALL THINGS

If God were not able to have control over all time and He lacked the ability to carry out His plans, what would that tell us about Him?

What does the fact that God is, in fact, totally sovereign say about Him?

How do we benefit from the fact God is in total control of

the what, when, and where of all things? Try to come up with at least five benefits:

1.

2.

3.

4.

5.

The Perfect Moment...

God determined the perfect moment for creation, the flood, the birth of Abraham's son Isaac, the birth of Jesus, the time of Jesus' ministry, the crucifixion, sending the Holy Spirit, and for all future events.

What are some examples of how you personally have seen God's perfect timing manifest in your life?

If from your perspective something does *not* appear to happen in a timely manner, how should you respond?

THE HOLY SPIRIT GIVES US THE ABILITY TO UNDERSTAND GOD'S TIMES

What purpose did the prophets serve, according to Amos 3:7?

What does 2 Peter 1:20-21 say is the ultimate source of every "prophecy of Scripture"?

In Matthew 16:2-3, why did Jesus rebuke the Jewish religious leaders of His day?

Why does it make sense for us to pay careful attention to what the Spirit tells us in Scripture if we want to "discern the signs of the times" (Matthew 16:3)?

When the disciples asked Jesus "Lord, will you at this time restore the kingdom to Israel?" (Acts 1:6), how did He respond? That is, what focus did He give them (Acts 1:7-8; see page 110 in *Israel and the Church*)?

WE ARE TO USE TIME WISELY WHILE TIME IS STILL AROUND TO BE USED

With regard to the Lord's return, why is it so urgent that we always be ready, according to 1 Thessalonians 5:1-3?

With that in mind, what does 1 Peter 4:7-11 say about how we are to live? Find at least four exhortations in this passage:

1.

2.

3.

4.

> "While we still quite literally have time, Peter tells us to be about God's business. We are called to live the way we should live—to be serious and watchful, not frivolous and self-focused. Ours should be sacrificial lives of love, sharing with others the physical and spiritual blessings given to us by the Holy Spirit."
>
> *Israel and the Church*, page 113

Taking This Lesson to Heart

What truth or principle had the greatest impact on you in chapter 6 of *Israel and the Church*?

What do you appreciate most about the fact God has total control over *what* happens, and *when*?

In what ways do you believe you can improve on your use of time? As you answer this question, come up with two or three "action items" you can do right away.

Spend some moments now in prayer, asking the Lord to (1) help you place greater trust in His timing for everything in your life, and (2) enable you to make wise use of the time you have left in life.

PART 3:

TWO PATHS IN REVELATION

THE BEGINNING
OF THE END

> "All creation is moving minute by minute, day by day, to a time when time is no more. But not all paths to that final destination are the same. Israel has one path, the church has another, and those who are not a part of either Israel or the church have a third. In these next chapters, we will focus on God's plans for Israel and the church. While these two tracks are separate right now, there is coming a time when they will converge for a while before finally merging into one. As our roadmap for these two routes, we will use the book of Revelation."

Israel and the Church, page 117

When it comes to the book of Revelation, many people know only a vague, sketchy outline of what it contains. They know about all the terrible judgments God will pour out on the earth. They know that the Antichrist is a key figure, and they know that in the end, Christ will return and instantaneously defeat all His enemies as He descends upon the Mount of Olives. But because there is so much action going on in Revelation, and because there is a lot of controversy over how certain passages should be interpreted, many people shy away from getting to know the book. They assume it is too difficult to understand. It doesn't help that many pastors and their churches are reluctant to study Revelation. For this reason, there is a lot of confusion about what will take place in the future.

Tragically, this means two very important subjects in the Bible are overlooked: Israel and the church. Both have key places in the book of Revelation. And it's not until we have a clear understanding of what happens to Israel and the church during the last days that we will gain a clear picture of God's plans for the future.

That is our goal in the next four chapters—to take a closer look at Israel and the church in Revelation.

KEY FACTS ABOUT THE BOOK OF REVELATION

According to preterists, when was the book of Revelation written?

What horrible historical event do preterists say is in view in Revelation?

Read the following passages in Revelation. Do these appear to describe a *local* Roman conquest and destruction of Jerusalem (as claimed by preterists), or do they better fit a scenario involving *global* destruction—thus demonstrating the prophecies in Revelation have not been fulfilled yet?

Revelation 9:18—

Revelation 13:3—

Revelation 16:3—

Revelation 16:4—

Revelation 16:8-9—

Revelation 16:14—

There are additional passages that fit better with a world-wide destruction rather than a local one. But the sampling serves as evidence that the horrors described in the book of Revelation do not match the destruction that took place in Rome's conquest of Jerusalem in AD 70.

What is the foundational premise of Replacement Theology?

What are the reasons that a late date for the writing of Revelation makes more sense than an early date (see pages 119-122 in *Israel and the Church*)?

What are some evidences that affirm the apostle John is the author of Revelation?

In Revelation 1:3, what promise is given to the person who reads the book of Revelation?

Why would Satan prefer we not read Revelation?

A PREVIEW OF WHAT IS TO COME

Why would God want to reveal to us what is to come?

According to the following passages, how should the possibility that Christ could return at any time affect the way we live?

1 Thessalonians 5:4-6,11—

Hebrews 9:24-25—

2 Peter 3:11-12—

1 John 3:2-3—

THE MESSENGER AND THE MESSAGE

What nickname did Jesus give to the brothers James and John, and what does the nickname mean?

What took place in Luke 9:54 that confirms how fitting this nickname was for James and John?

What evidences do we see that John had a deep love for Jesus?

According to Revelation 1:4, to whom did John write the book of Revelation?

How does John describe the Lord Jesus Christ in Revelation 1:13-16?

How did John respond upon seeing Christ (verse 17)?

What three things did Jesus ask John to write (verse 19)? (Here, we see Jesus give John the outline for the book of Revelation.)

One key reason people shy away from reading the book of Revelation is that it includes some symbolic language. However, if we look carefully, we'll discover that frequently, the symbolic language can be clearly understood—either in Revelation itself, or by looking to other Scripture passages. Let's look at an example of this in Revelation chapter 1.

What did John see Jesus "in the midst of" in verse 13?

What did Jesus have in His right hand in verse 16?

How were the "mysteries" in verses 13 and 16 explained in verse 20?

This one example confirms that, with careful attention, we

can figure out much of the seemingly complex language in Revelation—and therefore understand this book!

> "Then John felt a touch. Imagine that moment. It had been sixty years since he had felt a touch from that hand. It was a touch of love, of peace, of grace and blessing and strength sufficient to fortify his old bones to endure the journey that lay ahead. Jesus spoke again, this time softer: 'Do not be afraid; I am the First and the Last. I am He who lives, and was dead, and behold, I am alive forevermore. Amen. And I have the keys of Hades and of Death' (Revelation 1:17-18). John likely would have sat up as Jesus explained why He had come. 'I have a job for you. I want you to write down what you're about to see.'"
>
> *Israel and the Church*, page 128

Taking This Lesson to Heart

What truth or principle had the greatest impact on you in chapter 7 of *Israel and the Church*?

Based on what you have learned about Revelation so far, how can we benefit from reading this book?

First John 3:2-3 says,

> Beloved, now we are children of God; and it has not yet been revealed what we shall be, but we know that when He is revealed, we shall be like Him, for we shall see Him as He is. And everyone who has this hope in Him purifies himself, just as He is pure.

Why should living in the expectation of Christ's return have a purifying effect on us?

Take time to pray and ask, "Search me, O God, and know my heart...and see if there is any wicked way in me" (Psalm 139:23-24). Ask the Lord to help you be a vessel He can use as we draw closer to the end times.

THE CHURCH
IN REVELATION

"Jesus dictated and John wrote, and out of this great collaborative duo came seven brief but amazing letters. What did this process look like? It's hard to know because John suspended his narration for a time. Rather than giving us a glimpse into the writing process, he simply delivered us the result—missives from God directed toward seven key churches in an area that is currently part of southern Turkey."

Israel and the Church, page 131

Revelation chapters 2 and 3 are comprised of letters from Jesus that were written to seven churches in the cities of Ephesus, Smyrna, Pergamos, Thyatira, Sardis, Philadelphia, and Laodicea. While these were seven historical churches that actually existed, the positive and negative issues Jesus addresses in His letters have continued to be found in churches all through the ages and are present in churches today. This tells us that what Christ says to these ancient congregations is relevant for all time. For this reason, the commendations and warnings from Jesus should be heeded by every believer today.

EPHESUS—THE LOST LOVE

Read Revelation 2:2-3. For what reasons did Christ commend those in the church at Ephesus?

What warning did Jesus give in verses 4-5?

How would you characterize your relationship with Christ—is your love for Him what it should be? Where is there room for growth?

What word of hope did the Lord give to the Ephesian church (see verse 7)?

SMYRNA—THE ATTRACTIVENESS OF SUFFERING

What praise did Jesus give to the believers in Smyrna (Revelation 2:9-10)?

What two kinds of persecution were these Christians enduring (verses 9-10)?

What assurances do we find in Scripture that can comfort us when we suffer?

Romans 5:3-4—

Hebrews 13:5-6—

1 Peter 5:10—

What promise did Jesus give to the believers in Smyrna in verses 10-11?

PERGAMUM—DEFENDING THE TRUTH IN A CULTURE OF LIES

Read Revelation 2:12-13. What commendation did Christ give to the Christians in Pergamum in verse 13?

What problem did Jesus point out in verses 14-15?

When we as Christians ignore the Word of God, sin will eat away at us. What benefits do we gain when we make Scripture a priority in our lives?

Psalm 119-11—

2 Timothy 3:16-17—

1 Peter 2:1-2—

What corrective action did the Lord command the church to take in verse 16?

THYATIRA—FINDING A MORAL COMPASS

What good qualities did Jesus commend in the Christians at Thyatira (Revelation 2:19)?

What warning did the Lord give in verses 20-23, and why?

Why is sexual sin so dangerous?

What reward does Jesus promise to those who don't compromise (see verses 26-28)?

SARDIS—REVIVING
A DEAD CHURCH

According to Revelation 3:1, what assessment did Christ give of the church at Sardis?

Though the people in the church were not indulging in sin, they were dead and unresponsive to Christ. Read the passages below. What do we as believers need to do to maintain strong spiritual health?

John 15:4-5—

Romans 12:1-2—

Galatians 5:16-17—

What multiple commands did Jesus give to those in the church at Sardis (Revelation 3:2-4)?

PHILADELPHIA—FIND US FAITHFUL

In what ways did Jesus praise the church at Philadelphia (Revelation 3:8-9)?

What promise does the Lord give to these believers in verse 10?

Note that Jesus commended the people for keeping His "command to persevere" (verse 10). Read the following passages. For the Christian, what does perseverance look like?

Romans 5:3-4—

Romans 12:12—

Galatians 6:9—

James 1:2-4—

What does the "hour of trial" refer to?

What command and reward does Christ promise to this church in verses 11-12?

LAODICEA—THE CHURCH THAT MAKES JESUS SICK

What rebuke did Jesus give to the church at Laodicea, and why (Revelation 3:15-16)?

What attitude did the people in the church have, according to verse 17?

What are some ways we can make sure we don't fall into apathy and complacency?

What commands does Jesus give in verses 18-20?

"The Western church is wealthy and comfortable, and, as such, is to a large extent dangerously lukewarm. This is because so many have bought into the world's temporal mindset. Life is all about the material stuff and living in the here and now. It is when our eyes are opened to the spiritual that we see the desperate need in which we are living. How can we keep our eyes on the spiritual so that we don't fall into apathy and complacency—a vomit-inducing lukewarmness? The spiritual perspective will come only as we spend time in the Bible and on our knees in prayer. These tools will aid us in blocking out the worthless and focusing on the priceless."

Israel and the Church, pages 148-149

Taking This Lesson to Heart

What truth or principle had the greatest impact on you in chapter 8 of *Israel and the Church*?

In the letters to the seven churches, Christ was very forthright about any negative qualities He saw. Why is it so important that we as believers are committed to purity and perseverance?

If Christ were to write a letter to you, what would He say? Take time to carefully consider that question in prayer, asking God to reveal (1) what you need to let go of, and (2) what you need to hold fast to.

ISRAEL IN REVELATION—PART 1

"As we enter chapter 4, we come to a big shift in time. Chapters 2 and 3 centered on the church as it was in the first century. Jesus affirmed, challenged, and condemned the churches based on their successes, struggles, and sins. Certainly there were elements that were forward-looking, particularly with His repetition of promises of future rewards for those who overcome. There was also a timeless quality to many of Jesus' admonitions and affirmations—words that are as true for the church today as they were for the first-century church. But once chapter 4 begins, John is taken into a time that is yet to come."

Israel and the Church, page 151

What shift in time occurs as we enter Revelation chapter 4?

REVELATION 4:
A JOURNEY TO HEAVEN

What does John behold in Revelation 4:2-3?

What does he hear (verses 8 and 11)?

What is never mentioned from Revelation chapter 4 all the way to chapter 19, and why?

What do the following passages say about the rapture of the church, which will take place before the tribulation?

John 14:1-3—

1 Corinthians 15:51-52—

1 Thessalonians 4:13-17—

Revelation 3:10—

REVELATION 5:
THE LION AND THE LAMB

Who was the only one worthy to open the seven-sealed scroll (Revelation 5:5)?

For what reason was this worthy one said to be qualified to break the seals (verses 9-10)?

What was the Lamb said to be worthy of receiving (verse 12)?

REVELATION 6: THE
BEGINNING OF TROUBLES

What four creatures were released when the first four seals were broken, and what do they bring with them (Revelation 6:2-8)?

1.

2.

3.

4.

For what two reasons will God bring the tribulation to the earth?

The Gentile reason—

The Jewish reason—

What is the significance of the tribulation being called the time of *Jacob's* trouble (Jeremiah 30:7) and not the time of the *church's* trouble?

Why is the breaking of the fifth seal a bittersweet revelation?

The bitter aspect—

The sweet aspect—

REVELATION 7: TRIBULATION EVANGELISM

What is the first group of people we meet in Revelation 7 (see verses 4-8)?

What is the second group, and how is it described in verse 9?

"Notice the identity of the primary evangelists of the tribulation. It is not the church. God had to look elsewhere to find His workforce. Why? Because the church is gone. His chosen sealed-with-the-Spirit servants are already with Him in heaven, so He turns to His original chosen servants and seals them on their foreheads (verse 3). Israel was the first who were given the role of being a light to the nations. When they rejected their mission, the assignment was passed on to the church. Once the church is taken away, the responsibility of pointing the world to God will return to Israel. Two peoples, two roles—both loved and used by God."

Israel and the Church, page 164

REVELATION 8:
ECOLOGICAL DISASTERS

What happened after each of the first four trumpets were sounded?

1.

2.

3.

4.

All four of the judgments above demonstrate God's power over the natural world. What one or two other incidents in Scripture can you think of that also exhibit the Lord's control over nature?

REVELATION 9: A HUMAN HOLOCAUST

What is released when the fifth trumpet sounds (Revelation 9:3)?

Which people will they avoid (verse 4)?

Which people will they attack, and what will be the result (verses 4-6)?

What was released when the sixth trumpet sounded, and what percentage of mankind was killed (verses 14-18)?

Read verses 20-21. What will be the response of those who are not killed by this judgment?

What does this tell you about the hardness of unbelievers' hearts, even though it's very clear to them God is the source of the warnings and judgments?

"When we write off sin in our lives or the lives of others as no big deal, we need to remember this mind-boggling number [of deaths during the tribulation]. Sin is rebellion against the Creator. It is expressing to Him that we are going to do things our way and not His. It is telling Him that we are our own god, and He can take His Bible and His rules and go pound sand. Sin—no matter how big or small—matters."

Israel and the Church, page 166

Taking This Lesson to Heart

What truth or principle had the greatest impact on you in chapter 9 of *Israel and the Church*?

While God's wrath is a major theme in Revelation, God's mercy is too. Consider the 144,000 witnesses for Christ who will bring the gospel to "a great multitude no one could number" (Revelation 7:1-15), the two witnesses in Jerusalem who will have a worldwide stage (11:3), and the angel who will proclaim the "eternal gospel to…every nation" (14:6-7). In what ways do you recall experiencing God's mercy while you were still an unbeliever?

Repeatedly in Revelation, we see angelic and other creatures worshipping God without ceasing. What is the state of your worship—where is there room for growth? Why is it good for you to engage in worship habitually? Take time now to pray to—and worship—God.

ISRAEL IN REVELATION—PART 2

"When sin entered the world, death came with it. This included spiritual death, which resulted in mankind's separation from a holy God, and physical death, which led to a deterioration of all of creation."

Israel and the Church, page 182

REVELATION 10:
A BITTERSWEET MOMENT

What was John to do with the book offered to him by the angel (Revelation 10:8-9)?

What does this book represent, and what made it both sweet and bitter?

Read Psalm 19:7-11. In what ways is God's Word sweet to those who look to it for help?

Read Romans 9:1-5. To what extent did the apostle Paul grieve for His fellow Jews who had rejected Christ?

What can we as Christians do to ensure we have this same kind of love and concern for unbelievers?

REVELATION 11: JERUSALEM'S PREACHERS AND EARTHQUAKE

What will the two witnesses in Revelation 11:3 do?

What protection will God give to the two witnesses (verse 5)?

What special powers will the two witnesses have (verse 6)?

These two witnesses will be Jewish and will proclaim God's messages of salvation and judgment primarily to a Jewish nation, as well as to the world. What does the fact God will protect them—and more importantly, their messages—for 1,260 days tell you about God's desire to reach unbelievers?

REVELATION 12:
THE NATION THAT WON'T DIE

How is God's protection of the nation of Israel portrayed in Revelation 12:1-6 and verse 14 (hint: the woman represents Israel)?

Read Exodus 19:4. How is this similar to what we read about in Revelation 12:14?

According to Zechariah 13:9, what is God's ultimate purpose for Israel during the tribulation (see also Zechariah 12:10)?

REVELATION 13: ANTICHRIST
ONE AND TWO

How will the world respond to the Antichrist (Revelation 13:3-4)?

The Antichrist will be accompanied by a second beast, or the false prophet. What will this false prophet do (verses 12-14)?

What restriction will be placed on all people around the globe (verses 16-17)?

REVELATION 14:
EVANGELISM EXPLOSION

In the following verses, what can we learn about God's 144,000 Jewish witnesses who will proclaim the gospel worldwide?

Verse 1—

Verse 4—

Verse 5—

These witnesses will be unswervingly loyal to Christ. What kind of loyalty are we called to as Christ-followers?

Matthew 16:24—

John 12:26—

Read Revelation 14:12-13. What does this reveal to us in terms of how difficult it will be for the 144,000 to carry out their ministry?

REVELATION 15: THE PAUSE
THAT REFRESHES

Who breaks forth in song in Revelation 15:2, and what do they proclaim (see verses 3-4)?

Note especially that they sing "just and true are Your ways." Do you agree that God's judgments are just and fair? Why?

REVELATION 16: THE ROAD
TO ARMAGEDDON

The first five bowl judgments unleash horrendous judgments upon the world. How will people respond, according to Revelation 16:9, 11?

This response shouldn't surprise us—what does Scripture say people will be like in the last days, according to 2 Timothy 3:1-5?

REVELATION 17–18: COLLAPSE OF THE WORLDWIDE RELIGION AND BANKRUPTCY OF THE WORLD ECONOMY

What do we witness in Revelation 17?

What do we see destroyed in Revelation 18?

How long will it take for this judgment to occur (see Revelation 18:17)? What does this tell you about the extent of God's sovereignty and power?

REVELATION 19: A WONDERFUL WEDDING

From Revelation chapters 4–18, we follow what happens to Israel and unbelievers during the tribulation. Where does the apostle John shift to in chapter 19?

What do we see being celebrated in verses 1-6?

While there's great sadness in seeing God's judgment poured out upon the wicked, why should this also bring us great joy?

In verses 11-16, we read about Christ's second coming—during which the church will follow Him to earth to destroy His enemies. What inspires you most about Christ's promised return?

REVELATION 20: PLANET EARTH UNDER NEW MANAGEMENT

According to Revelation 20:1-3, what is the first order of events as Christ sets up His 1,000-year kingdom (also known as the millennial kingdom)?

In Revelation 20:1-10 we read about the millennial kingdom. According to the following passages, what will life be like in this kingdom?

Isaiah 11:6-9—

Ezekiel 34:26-27—

Micah 4:3—

What will happen at the end of the millennial kingdom (Revelation 20:7-9)?

Who will be present at the Great White Throne judgment, and what will happen to them (verses 11-15)?

REVELATION 21: BACK TO THE DRAWING BOARD

At this time, God will make "all things new" (Revelation 21:5). Read verses 1-7. What appeals to you most about what life will be like in the new heaven and new earth?

What are the major features of the new Jerusalem, according to verses 22-27?

REVELATION 22: READY OR NOT, HERE I COME

"This last chapter of Revelation looks back on the Lord's promise to return for His own. In a way, the last chapter brings us back to our time—to our reality—and it speaks of the love of God, the hope for the believer, the wages of sin, which is death, and, of course, the free gift of eternal life. It speaks of prophecy revealed in the book and the urgency of our task as Christ's ambassadors. Jesus said, 'Behold, I am coming quickly! Blessed is he who keeps the words of the prophecy of this book' (Revelation 22:7)."

Israel and the Church, page 183

What four things are you looking forward to most about life in eternity?

1.

2.

3.

4.

Taking This Lesson to Heart

What truth or principle had the greatest impact on you in chapter 10 of *Israel and the Church*?

Do you feel ready for Christ's return and reign? What can you do to put yourself in a greater state of readiness?

Scripture gives us only a small glimpse of what life will be like in eternity. Our future will be far more glorious than we can imagine. Take time now to pray and thank the Lord for all that awaits you in your heavenly home.

PART 4:

TWO PEOPLES, ONE FAMILY

LESSON 11

WHO GOES WHERE?

"Few questions are more important than those about the afterlife because death, for all of us, is essentially right around the corner. Where do we go when we die? Some are asking this question because they've lost their parents. Some are asking about what will happen to nonbelievers they know. Some are curious about what happened to Old Testament people compared to those they read about in the New Testament. There are even those who are desperate to know where their dearly departed pets are. If this last one includes you, I need to let you know up front that this book will not give you the answer as to where your emotional support pony is dwelling now that it's eaten its last sugar cube.

"What is next for us once this life is over? And what about all those who have gone before?"

Israel and the Church, page 188

ALL WAS GOOD—UNTIL THE FALL

After God was finished with all creation, what did He say about it in Genesis 1:31?

Early on, Adam and Eve were able to enjoy perfect, intimate fellowship with God. What broke the fellowship?

God is the source of all life and righteousness. What, then, is the result of being *separated* from life and righteousness?

Though mankind rebelled against God, what was the Lord's response, according to the following passages?

Romans 5:8—

Ephesians 2:1-7—

DEATH IS NOT THE END

What does Hebrews 9:27 say happens to every person without exception?

What is the benefit of living with the expectation that the rapture or death could happen at any time?

THE FUTURE PLAN FOR ISRAEL

A Time of Trouble Is Coming

What will happen to Israel, according to the following passages?

Daniel 12:1—

Matthew 24:21—

Revelation 12:12-17—

What will be the two destinies of the people who endure the tribulation (verses 2-3)?

The Resurrection Is Coming

In Luke 20:37-38, what did Jesus point to as evidence that ultimately, everyone will be resurrected?

What else did Jesus say about the afterlife?

John 3:18—

John 11:25-26—

John 14:1-3—

GOD MAKES THE PLANS

The First and Second Births

What does Scripture say is true about our spiritual state at our first birth?

Psalm 51:5—

Ephesians 5:12—

How is the second birth described in John 5:24?

In 2 Corinthians 5:17?

In Titus 3:4-5?

The First and Second Deaths

What is the first death?

Why should unbelievers fear the first death?

TWO KINDS OF PEOPLE,
TWO DESTINIES

What is the second death?

What is the only thing that can spare us from the second death, and why?

John 5:24—

Revelation 1:18—

When will the next resurrection take place, and who will be taken up?

Who will be resurrected at the second coming of Christ?

WHICH PLACE WILL YOU BE IN?

"Paul wrote to the church in Rome, 'If you confess with your mouth the Lord Jesus and believe in your heart that God has raised Him from the dead, you will be saved. For with the heart one believes unto righteousness, and with the mouth confession is made unto salvation' (Romans 10:9-10)…if you truly believe that Jesus is who He has said He is—the promised Messiah, God Himself—and you commit to Him as your Lord, the one you will strive to follow all your life, you will be saved from the second death and the second resurrection. Your eternity will be secure. You will forever enjoy the company of the Creator God in His new heaven and new earth."

Israel and the Church, pages 205-206

According to the following passages, once we are saved, how secure is our eternal destination?

John 10:28-29—

Romans 8:1—

Romans 8:35-29—

Ephesians 1:13-14—

Taking This Lesson to Heart

What truth or principle had the greatest impact on you in chapter 11 of *Israel and the Church*?

Between the daily routines that keep us busy and the many distractions of everyday life, we rarely think about the sobering reality that life on earth is fleeting (James 4:14). How much of your time and energy is devoted to the things that truly count for eternity? In what areas of your life is there room for improvement?

Read Matthew 6:19-21 and Colossians 3:1-2. Spend some time in prayer now and ask the Lord to (1) convict you about ways in which you fail to use your time well, and (2) give you greater wisdom about how you spend the rest of your life on earth so that it counts.

A SINISTER STRATEGY

"Now that we have the parallel yet distinct histories and futures of Israel and the church sorted out—now that we have seen clearly God's choice of His two peoples, His purposes for His two peoples, and His plans for His two peoples—it's time we come to an uncomfortable yet necessary question. Why throughout history has there been such a concerted global effort to, at the least, marginalize the Jewish people, and at most, to eradicate them altogether? To answer this question, we need to revisit the one who is leading the effort to shift Israel from 'chosen' status to 'forgotten' or 'forsaken.'"

Israel and the Church, page 207

Why is Satan so eager to destroy Israel?

SATAN'S STRATEGIES
AGAINST ISRAEL

Make the Nations Want to Get Rid of Israel

What are some historical examples of nations attempting to destroy Israel (see pages 209-214 in *Israel and the Church*)?

Based on what you see happening in today's world, what are some current examples of hatred toward Israel?

Make Christians Believe that God Is Done with Israel

What does Replacement Theology say about Israel?

What did the apostle Paul say about Israel in Romans 11:1-2?

What do the following passages say about the permanence of God's promises to Israel?

1 Samuel 12:22—

Psalm 89:31-37—

Make the Israelis Tired of Being Persecuted

Why does it make sense for Satan to wear out the people of Israel by making them be willing to pursue peace at any cost no matter what?

Do you agree that Israel's desire for peace will make them more vulnerable to the Antichrist's promise for peace—a promise that leads to the signing of a seven-year covenant (Daniel 9:27)? Why or why not?

ISRAEL AND THE CHURCH

What command does God give in Isaiah 40:1-2?

What important ministry has God gifted to all believers, according to 2 Corinthians 1:3-4?

Though we've looked at Genesis 12:1-3 earlier, let's look at it again. In this passage, who does God promise to bless?

What command and what promise is given in Psalm 122:6?

Taking This Lesson to Heart

What truth or principle had the greatest impact on you in chapter 12 of *Israel and the Church*?

What are some specific ways you have grown in your biblical awareness of Israel as a result of reading *Israel and the Church*?

With the previous question in mind, what are some ways you can be more active in praying for Israel and the Jewish people? Take some time to lift up these prayers now.

THE BLESSINGS
OF THE BLESSERS

"The Jews are God's chosen people. The church is God's chosen people...While we have emphasized the distinction between Israel and the church throughout this book, we must also recognize our interconnectedness. God has used Israel to announce Himself to the Gentile world, and He is using the church to draw Israel back to Himself."

Israel and the Church, page 228

THE CHURCH'S RESPONSIBILITY

What was Jesus' point when He told the story of the Good Samaritan (hint: see James 4:17)?

What should be true about all Christians, according to the passages on the next page?

1 Timothy 2:1—

James 2:8—

1 Peter 3:15—

We must keep in mind that the above commands include expressing compassion and love for the Jewish people.

TWO CHOSEN PEOPLES

Read Romans 11:28-32:

> Concerning the gospel they are enemies for your sake, but concerning the election they are beloved for the sake of the fathers. For the gifts and the calling of God are irrevocable. For as you were once disobedient to God, yet have now obtained mercy through their disobedience, even so these also have now been disobedient, that through the mercy shown you they also may obtain mercy. For God has committed them all to disobedience, that He might have mercy on all.

What does verse 28 say about "the election" of Israel?

What truth is clearly proclaimed in verse 29?

"God used Israel to announce Himself to the Gentile world, and He is using the church to draw Israel to Himself" (*The Church and Israel*, page 228). Do you agree with Romans 11:30-32 that God can use a person's sin to make His mercy all the more evident?

WHAT THE CHURCH SHOULDN'T DO

What is wrong with the idea of a dual covenant—that is, salvation by grace for Gentiles, and salvation by personal merit for Jews? What scriptures about salvation can you cite to support your answer?

Though perhaps well intended, what is faulty about the idea of Christians observing Jewish laws and festivals?

WHAT THE CHURCH SHOULD DO

Pray

What two prayers for Israel are found in Psalm 122:6-7?

What is the third reason that we, as Christians, should pray for Israel?

Proclaim

According to Romans 1:16, to whom is the gospel message for?

What helpful truth are we reminded of in Matthew 15:24?

Give

Think of some different ways that it is possible to show support for the Jewish people, and list them below.

A MARVELOUS PROMISE

Lamentations 3:22-23 says,

> Through the LORD's mercies we are not consumed,
> Because His compassions fail not.
> They are new every morning;
> Great is Your faithfulness (Lamentations 3:22-23).

As a result of reading *Israel and the Church*, in what ways have you seen God's faithfulness affirmed?

"God will never leave nor forsake that which is His own. As a Jew, I receive great comfort from knowing that He has not forgotten my people, and that in the end, He will draw them to Himself. And, as a believing member of God's church, I derive great comfort from knowing that the same God who will not abandon Israel will not abandon me—no matter what my faults or failures may be."

Israel and the Church, page 234

Taking This Lesson to Heart

What truth or principle had the greatest impact on you in chapter 13 of *Israel and the Church*?

As a result of reading chapter 13, write at least four different ideas that come to mind about *why* and *how* you can support Israel.

1.

2.

3.

4.

What are you most grateful for as a result of reading *Israel and the Church*? Take time to give your answer in the form of a heartfelt prayer to God.